François-Joseph Fétis

How to Pay from Score

Treatise on aAccompaniment from Score on the Organ or Pianoforte

François-Joseph Fétis

How to Pay from Score
Treatise on aAccompaniment from Score on the Organ or Pianoforte

ISBN/EAN: 9783744783880

Printed in Europe, USA, Canada, Australia, Japan

Cover: Foto ©Thomas Meinert / pixelio.de

More available books at **www.hansebooks.com**

TREATISE ON ACCOMPANIMENT

FROM SCORE

ON THE

ORGAN OR PIANOFORTE.

BY

F. J. FETIS.

TRANSLATED BY

ALFRED WHITTINGHAM.

London:
WILLIAM REEVES, 83, CHARING CROSS ROAD, W.C.

CONTENTS.

———

TREATISE ON ACCOMPANIMENT
FROM SCORE

ON THE

ORGAN OR PIANOFORTE.

*I*NTRODUCTION.

IF it were only possible to hear the productions of the great composers by means of a complete orchestra they would be very little known ; the taste for music would be less universal, and the progress of this art would be much slower. But a valuable instrument, an instrument which offers all the harmonic resources of a collection of different instruments, which has over the orchestra the advantage of unity and spontaneity of intention, and which often rivals it in effect when it is touched by a skilful accompanist—the Pianoforte,—happily frees us from our embarrassment and from the expense which the collection of a great number of musicians in the same place would involve.

B

Ranged round a Pianoforte, the singers perceive much more easily the time, when they take it from a single accompanist, than when they are obliged to discern it in the midst of all the shades of movement between which the instrumentalists vacillate. With any degree of intelligence, he who is seated at the piano and has the score before his eyes perceives at once the hesitation of a singer, and guides him, or helps him in an insensible manner, by allowing him to hear the intonation, by holding him back, by pressing him on, and sometimes by conforming himself to his intentions. All this cannot be done by an orchestra except after a considerable amount of uncertainty and fluctuation, which are really only so many faults in the execution.

2. But inasmuch as the functions of the accompanist are onerous, so they require in him good natural ability and solid knowledge. It is necessary that he should be a skilful·reader, that all the clefs should be familiar to him, that he should possess sufficient mechanical power over the instrument not to be stopped by any difficulties which he may happen to encounter, that he should have intelligence and tact in order to choose in the score that which can with the greatest advantage be produced upon the Pianoforte, that the feeling of harmony which he has received from nature should have been developed by sound study, and that long practice should have revealed to him the style most fitted to each kind of music.

3. It will be perceived that it is not my object in this work to treat of the principles of music, of the fingering of the piano, nor of harmony itself: these are matters which may fairly be supposed to have been acquired before anyone thinks of studying the art of accompaniment, which is but the application of them. It is this art of accompaniment that I wish to teach, and for this reason I shall only speak of those preliminaries which directly concern it.

FIRST SECTION.—Preliminaries.

Chapter I.

Of the different arrangements of voices and instruments in Scores (Partitions).

4. The musician who undertakes the composition of a Symphony, a Concerto, an Opera, or any work for several voices or for several instruments, cannot realize the effect which should result until he has under his eyes all the parts which run together. The method to be followed for this is very simple : it consists in writing on a different staff of each page that which is given to each voice or to each instrument, and uniting these staves by a brace and by bars drawn perpendicularly. This union of different parts is called a Score (Partition).

5. Scores are absolutely necessary to the conductors of Orchestras and of Choirs, also to directors of Concerts, and indispensable to accompanists ; for it is only by their means that an idea can be formed of the effect of the Composition as a whole, and of the effect of the passages assigned to different voices or to different instruments.

6. Composers do not all arrange their scores in the same manner. Each one has his method, the choice of which, being indifferent, is first determined

by caprice and becomes afterwards a matter of habit. There are nevertheless certain rules of arrangement which have been generally adopted and which are conformable to reason. Thus the voices range them-selves in the order which they occupy in the general system of octaves, the lowest at the foot of the page, from which the others gradually ascend.

EXAMPLES.

Arrangement of a Chorus of 4 Voices.	1st Arrangement of a Chorus of 5 Voices.	2nd Arrangement of a Chorus of 5 Voices.
1. Soprano.	1. Soprano.	1. Soprano.
2. Contralto.	2. Mezzo-Soprano.	2. Soprano.
3. Tenor.	3. Contralto.	1. Tenor.
4. Bass.	4. Tenor.	2. Tenor.
	5. Bass.	3. Bass.

When the Partition is for two, three, or four Choirs, the voices are arranged as follows :—

1st Choir.
Soprano.
Contralto.
Tenor.
Bass.

2nd Choir.
Soprano.
Contralto.
Tenor.
Bass.

In a piece in several parts as a Quintett, Sextett, or Finale, all the parts or voices of the same kind are braced together : thus all the Sopranos, all the Tenors, and all the Basses are placed upon adjoining staves.

7. The method generally adopted for the arrangement of vocal pieces with orchestral accompaniment is to place all the instrumental above the vocal parts with the exception of the bass, which is placed beneath.

8. I have remarked (6) that the arrangement of the parts in the score is ordered by the fancy of the composer; this is specially true in all that concerns instrumental music. In ancient compositions this arrangement was always the same, because the orchestra was only composed of Violins, Tenors, and Basses. As the number and quality of instruments increased it was necessary to make other arrangements: then it was that every one did that which appeared to him the most convenient.

But among all the varieties, some were more generally adopted than others. These were: 1. Those in which the Violins and Tenors were placed at the top, and were followed by the Wind Instruments classed according to their degree of elevation in the general scale of sounds, with the Violoncellos and Basses on the lower staves. 2. Those in which the wind instruments, beginning with the Flute, were placed at the top of the page, and were followed by the Violins, Tenors, Violoncellos, and Basses. 3. Those in which the instruments of percussion and the brass instruments, such as Kettle-drums, Trumpets, Horns, and Trombones, were succeeded by the Flutes, Hautboys, Clarionettes, Bassoons, Violins, Tenors, and Basses. The first of these arrangements is that of the greater part of the Italian masters and of Mozart. The second is the manner of the French School, M. Cherubini, Beethoven, &c. Several works of Haydn present specimens of the third arrangement.

EXAMPLES of the three principal arrangements of Scores (Partitions).

1st Arrangement.	2nd Arrangement.	3rd Arrangement.
1st Violin.	Flutes.	Kettle-drums.
2nd Violin.	Oboes.	Trumpets.
Alto.	Clarionets.	Horns.
Flutes.	Horns.	Trombones.
Oboes.	Trumpets.	Flutes.
Clarionets.	Bassoons.	Oboes.
Horns.	Trombones.	Clarionets.
Trumpets.	Kettle-drums.	Bassoons.
Bassoons.	1st Violin.	1st Violin.
Trombones.	2nd Violin.	2nd Violin.
Kettle-drums.	Alto.	Alto.
Violoncello.	Violoncello.	Violoncello.
Double Bass.	Double Bass.	Double Bass.

9. The search after new effects has caused the multiplication of instruments in these latter days, but those which have been added form part of one or another of the classes above mentioned. The small Flutes (Piccolos) are classified with ordinary Flutes ; the Ophicleides and Keyed Trumpets with the Brass Instruments ; the Triangles, Cymbals, and Great Drum are placed with the Kettle-drums.

10. The worst arrangement is that in which the Wind Instruments separate the Tenor Violin from the Violoncello; it breaks the Quartett of Stringed

Instruments, which, being of far greater importance than the rest, ought to be kept together so that the accompanist may perceive the whole at a glance. This arrangement is frequently to be found in the scores of Gluck, in which the Alto part is almost always to be found immediately above the voices, without regard to the place occupied by the Violins.

11. The Italian Scores have always the same number of Staves in the course of a piece; in France the engravers, for the sake of economising space, suppress those staves which appertain to the instruments which remain silent. This continual variation in the number of staves braced together is a source of some difficulty to inexperienced accompanists; but after a little practice the matter becomes easy enough.

It is necessary to notice the names of the instruments which are placed at the commencement of the staves; by this means we avoid all uncertainty.

CHAPTER II.

On Vocal Parts ; Instrumental Parts; their Fixed Pitch and the manner in which they are written.

12. Each voice, each instrument, has its extent and its limits from grave to acute. It is this extent, these limits and other matters, which I shall presently explain, these determine the choice of the clefs which should be employed in writing.

13. All Voices, in which are included the varieties of each species, may be reduced to seven ; viz., 1. The Soprano. 2. The Mezzo Soprano. 3. The Contralto (a low-pitched female voice, very rare in France). 4. The High Tenor. 5. The Tenor. 6. The Baritone. 7. The Bass.

14. In Italy the C clef placed upon the first line is employed for the Soprano, Mezzo Soprano, and Contralto Voices, but in France the Soprano is often written with the G clef. This is more conformable to the intention of the Clefs, since by this means the use of the higher leger lines is avoided. When high Tenor Voices were less common, their part was written with the C clef on the third line. But since this kind of voice now finds its place amongst Tenors, that clef has disappeared from the greater part of Vocal Scores. All Tenor parts are written with the

C clef on the fourth line; the Mezzo Soprano or
Contralto is written with the C clef on the first line,
and has taken the place of the acute part of the Alto.

The F clef on the fourth line is used for the Baritone and Bass. It is as well to notice that some
authors have retained the C clef on the third line for
the Contralto in sacred music.

In this case a Chorus of four parts presents itself
under the following aspect :—Ex. 1.

15. The G clef on the second line is at present the
only one in use for Violins, Flutes, and Oboes.
These instruments play the same passages in unison,
with the exception of the Piccolo, which is naturally
an octave higher. Ex. 2.

16. The same clef is employed for the Clarionet
parts ; but these parts sometimes present difficulties
which it is as well to explain.

In the keys of C, F, G, A minor, D minor, and
E minor, the part for this instrument is written like
the Violin, Flute, or Oboe part, and is played in
unison with these instruments. But difficulties of
fingering and other small matters, which it is not
necessary to detail here, have caused the manu-
facture of particular Clarionets for the keys in which
sharps and flats are multiplied.

These Clarionets, which, from the respective length
of their tube, are a tone, or a tone and a half lower, or
an octave and a tone and a half, two tones and a half,
and three tones and a half higher than the written
note in the key of G, play always the notes just as

they are written; but the different lengths of the tube cause a natural transposition to which the executant need not pay attention.

The Clarionet a tone lower than the unison of the Violin, called the Clarionet in B flat, serves for the keys of B flat, E flat, A flat, G minor, C minor, and F minor.

The Clarionet in A is that which is a tone and a half lower than the unison of the Violin. It serves for the key of D, A, E, B, B minor, F sharp minor, &c.

These are the instruments which are employed in ordinary orchestras; the others are only in use for military music or wind bands.

17. When Clarionet parts occur in a piece, the accompanist must examine whether the author has indicated by the words, Clarionet in C, Clarionet in B flat, or Clarionet in A, placed before the Clarionet parts in the Score, the kind of Clarionet which he would have employed.

In the absence of any such indication it is necessary to consider the key of the piece and the manner in which the Clarionet part is written, in order to know whether it should be played in unison with the Violin, or whether a transposition is necessary.

If the Clarionet in B flat is in question, we imagine the C clef on the fourth line, and play a tone lower than that which is written. Ex. 3.

If the composer has used a Clarionet in A, the accompanist imagines the C clef on the first line, and plays a tone and a half lower. Ex. 4.

The Italian composers leave no room for sup-position. They write the clef of the transposition. Thus it is that in their Scores the key of C on the fourth line serves for the Clarionets in the keys of B flat and E flat ; but it should not be forgotten that all which is written for the Clarionet with this clef must be raised an octave ; this clef being that of the Tenor.   Ex. 5.

Everything written for the Clarionet in A, with the C clef on the first line must be executed at the real pitch of that clef.

18. The parts for the Alto Clarionet and Cor Anglais (a species of Oboe) which are naturally a fifth lower than the Clarionet in C, and the Oboe, are generally written with the G clef on the second line : but the accompanist makes a transposi-tion by imagining the clef C on the second line.   Ex. 6.

19. For the Bassoon two different clefs are used, according to the degree of gravity or elevation of the part.   The total extent of the instrument being from B flat below to the acute D ; it is manifest that it would be impossible to use the same clef for all the passages, except by multiplying leger lines to excess.   The clefs employed therefore, are those of F on the fourth line and C on the fourth line. When the part is written with the first, the instrument plays in unison with the Violoncello. When written with the other, the pitch is that of the Tenor.

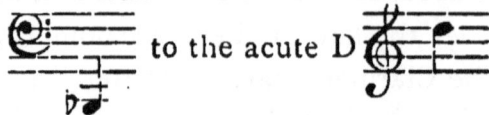

20. The instrumental parts in which transpositions are most frequently made are those of the Horns and Trumpets, because their construction is such that it is necessary to change the movable tubes which raise or lower the tone, without any necessity for the executant's occupying himself with the effect of this merely mechanical operation.

The parts for the Horns and Trumpets are therefore written in the key of C.

The indication of the key which the composer writes at the head of the piece makes the transposition evident.

For instance, these words,—Horns in D, in E flat, in F, indicate that the tonic C becomes D, or E flat, or F, and the accompanist imagines in his own mind the clef which is able to produce the indicated meta·morphosis.

21. But that no mistake may be made about the pitch at which the Horn passages should be reproduced on the pianoforte, it should be noted that in the key of C, that instrument is played an octave lower than the violin.   Ex. 7.

Thus all the keys on the Horn, with the exception of lower B flat, are taken rising, reckoning from the key of C.   Ex. 8.

22. The Horn parts are not always written in the key of the piece, possibly because certain keys not being in ordinary use, the ancient manufacturers did not consider them in the construction of the instrument: perhaps because the composer wished to obtain

certain effects which it would have been impossible to produce except by the employment of Horns in different keys; and perhaps for other reasons which it is not necessary that the accompanist should know.

For instance, the keys of A flat and B major never occurred in ancient parts for the Horn; they were supplied by parts in E flat and E major, which were more suited to them, and which offered a greater amount of resource.

As the Horns had no minor keys, the composer sometimes put one of these instruments in the major mode of the key of the piece, with the object of having at his command the principal notes of the scale, such as the Tonic, the Fourth, the Dominant, and put another horn in the relative major key of the key of the piece, so as to obtain the use of the Third and Sixth degree of the Minor Mode, and of all the notes of the relative major.   Ex 9.

Sometimes composers write two Horns in the major mode of the minor key, and two other Horns in the relative major key.   The richness of orchestration which has been adopted in these later days has caused use to be made of four Horns in the major keys.   In this case, there are two which are written in the key of the Tonic, and two in that of the Dominant.

It may be perceived after that which has been said, that the accompanist should make sure of the key in which the Horn parts are written before commencing a piece, and clearly perceive the operations necessary for their transposition.

23. I have already said that the Trumpet parts are written in the same manner as those of the Horns, and are transposed in the same manner ; but as this instrument is naturally an octave higher than the Horn in the key of C, it plays in unison with the parts of the Violin and Flute. Ex. 10.

In other keys, the instrument is gradually raised, so that it sounds another octave or two higher than is indicated by the clef of transposition. In D for example, the accompanist supposes the clef C on the third line, and plays an octave higher; in E flat, he imagines the clef F on the fourth line, and plays two octaves higher, and thus with the others.

24. The Trombone is rarely used alone. This instrument is divided into three kinds, to which are given the names of Bass Trombone, Tenor Trombone and Alto Trombone. Their parts are written in the clefs which belong to their denomination : thus the F clef serves for the Bass Trombone, the C clef on the fourth line for the Tenor Trombone, and the C clef on the third line for the Alto Trombone.

25. Each of these instruments being constructed in such a manner that all intonations can be executed upon them, it is never necessary to make any change in order to effect a change of key, and consequently the accompanist has never any transposition to make.

26. When three Trombones are employed, they are written on staves braced together. Ex. 11.

But sometimes want of space necessitates the three parts being written on the same line. Then the C clef on the fourth line is chosen, being the clef intermediate between the two others. Ex. 12.

27. Another new brass instrument, which, like the Trombone, is of various kinds, has lately passed from military music into the orchestra. This instrument is the Ophicleide, and its part is written in the same manner as that of the Trombone.

28. The method of writing for the Kettle-drums varies according to the authors. It is known that these instruments produce but one sound, and that in order to have by their means the Tonic and the Dominant, it is necessary to employ two instruments. Some authors write these two notes with the F clef, conforming to the key; thus, in the key of D, they write D, A; in E flat, B flat, &c. Others on the contrary content themselves with the indication by the words, Timbales in C, in D, in E flat, &c., the key of the piece, and write afterwards in C. The accompanist must make the transposition. Ex. 13.

28. The Great Drum, Cymbals and Triangle, having no well-determined intonation, have their part always written with one single note. The accompanist has never any occasion to reproduce them on the Pianoforte, such reproduction being impossible.

CHAPTER III.

Concerning the manner in which the Accompanist should read a Score in order to grasp its substance, and its details.

29. Nature sometimes prodigal, sometimes niggardly in her gifts, gives to certain individuals eyes which promptly grasp objects, and denies to others that faculty which is indispensable to a good accompanist.

The greater part of the Scores written before 1750 offer but little difficulty to the reader, because the orchestra is only composed of a small number of parts. Among the Italians, Carissimi, Scarlatti, and even Pergolesi, accompanied their vocal parts with two Violins and Bass only, for the Alto or Viola was combined almost always with the Bass.

But in proportion as simple forms went out of fashion, more complicated effects, and combinations of instruments more numerous became necessary ; thus the reading of scores has become each day more difficult. The richness of orchestration which composers employ at present makes their scores a labyrinth in which the inexperienced accompanist may well lose himself. It is therefore necessary that he should

c

habituate himself insensibly to these great difficulties
by the reading of simple works.

30. Upon opening a Score a skilful accompanist
sees at a glance everything upon the page which concerns himself, and discerns with the rapidity of
lightning that which should engage his attention, and
that which may be neglected. There are, in fact, in
the orchestra, certain instrumental parts which contain the most interesting passages of the accompaniment, together with others which are mere filling up.
Thus, considering the impossibility of reproducing
everything upon a Pianoforte, the accompanist is
obliged to choose that which is essential.

31. The first glance having been given, and the
choice of that which ought to be retained having been
made with promptitude, it is necessary to consider
quickly the details to which prominence should be
given. Several things tend to facilitate this examination. First : it is necessary to observe with precision
the order of the Score, so as not to confound the clefs
and the parts ; this is always easy in Italian or German Scores, but frequently presents great difficulties
in those of the French, in consequence of the custom
which the engravers have adopted of suppressing all
the parts which rest, in order to get as much as possible upon one page. And this is not all : In several
old Scores, notably those of the operas of Gluck‘
certain instruments, such as the Oboes, the Horns,
and the Bassoons, not having always staves to themselves, are written on those of the voices or of other

instruments when these rest.   Thus it becomes necessary to search for them, sometimes in one place
sometimes in another.   Ex. 14.

This is without doubt a great inconvenience, but it
is possible to become habituated to it and to render it
less irksome by preparing for it and, above all, by considering the habits of a composer and the epoch to
which he belongs.   It will be seen farther on that it
is necessary to a considerable extent to study the peculiar manner of each musician in order to become a
good accompanist.

32. The order of the Instruments in the Score being
known, it is necessary to have a sustained attention,
and to avoid everything which may distract the mind.
However, in certain cases harmonic knowledge, previously acquired, may prove a great assistance, and
greatly relieve the eyes.   For instance, sequences
and progressions of harmony, cadences, simple and
natural successions of chords, need not fix the
attention, but may allow it to wander in advance in
anticipation of that which follows.   Suppose that a
progression like the following should occur—Ex. 15.

From the second measure an accompanist who is a
harmonist will see that this is simply a progression of
common chords, chords of the sixth, and chords of $\frac{6}{4}$
which may be reduced to the following simple form :
Ex. 16.

And perceiving that this continues to the third
degree where the natural resolution occurs, his eye
will pass lightly over the rest of this progression and

will be cárried by anticipation to the fourth bar in
order to foresee the termination of the phrase.

33. When the form of the accompaniment has a
continued design, the eyes have no other occupation
than that of discovering the harmony and of applying
the design.   In this case the attention is not divided
between several objects, and has more liberty of reading in advance.   These fixed designs have also the
advantage of being so remarkable as to occupy the
ear exclusively and to permit the accompanist to neglect all other details.   From this it results that the
eye fixes itself, in cases like this, on two or three
parts, and simplifies its work.   Suppose, for example,
that anyone had to accompany the following passage
from Haydn's Imperial Mass.   Ex. 17.

At a glance it will be perceived that the design
commenced by the second Violin and continued by
the first, also the motion of the Bass, are the most important objects ; then, as this cannot be executed except by abandoning other parts, it is manifest that the
accompaniment of this passage should be read as in
the following example.   Ex. 18.

34. Though an exact knowledge of harmony is a
powerful auxiliary for the eye of the accompanist when
the music is well written, in some cases it renders no
assistance, especially in reading the music of some
particular composers.   For instance, Grétry had no
feeling for a good Bass, and often in his music the
progression of the parts is so perplexing that his resolutions are continually uncertain, and if the accom-

panist should make them in the regular way, there
would be great risk of serious error. Though apparently easy, this music would be difficult to read if it were
more heavily weighted with instrumental parts. It requires from the accompanist a more sustained attention
than other music, and it is necessary always to be
cautious about the apparent regularities of the cadences, and the resolutions of the harmony. I shall
give some examples, examining the style of accompaniments suited to each author.

35. Each author has certain forms which are
familiar to him, and which he frequently repeats
without perceiving the repetition. The frequent
recurrence of these forms is a clue which a skilful
accompanist learns to recognise, and which aids him
considerably in the reading of Scores.

There are also forms which appertain to certain
epochs of which they are characteristic. For instance,
with the exception of Bach, Handel, and Jomelli, few
composers before 1780 had made use of deceptive
cadences, or had terminated their phrases otherwise
than by the perfect cadence. This is a point of security for the accompanist. But when this epoch is
passed and we get to Mozart, it is necessary to be
more careful.

The eye can also rest with confidence on the instrumental quartet in all scores written during that epoch;
but in those of Mozart, and of all the composers who
have taken him for their model, the interest of the
accompaniment is as frequently found in the wind

instruments as in the others, and for a good accompaniment it is necessary to learn to cast the eyes with rapidity over the entire extent of the page.

In order to become insensibly accustomed to this, it is necessary for some time to read Scores without playing them; thus becoming habituated to hear the effect by simple reading, as if an orchestra were executing the piece under examination. This exercise appears to me to be one of the best possible.

36. Calmness is an indispensable quality in an accompanist. If that calmness should be lost, the eyes would be alarmed at the aspect of certain Scores which, full of notes and different designs, seem to present only an inextricable labyrinth, though generally this apparent multiplicity of motive is reduceable to a very simple matter, and easy of execution. With a calm eye and with reflection, the thought of the author is rapidly grasped, and that which ought to be transferred to the pianoforte is separated from that which requires no attention.

Frequently the parts are simply doubled in the octave or unison; the difference in the clefs alone gives an appearance of diversity to things which are identical, and a piece often appears extremely complicated which may be reduced to a harmony of three parts. Suppose, for example, that anyone had to accompany Beethoven's Mass (Op. 123), and had before him the following passage: Ex. 19.

At first sight it would seem that this page of Score is filled with an infinity of different parts; but it wil be perceived, upon an attentive examination, that the Flutes, the Oboes, and the Clarionets double the parts of the Violin either in the octave or in the unison; that the first Bassoon does the same thing as the alto Viola, and that the second is in unison with some of the Violoncello parts, and with portions of the Double Bass part. In fact that the whole is reduced, almost always, to an accompaniment in three parts, as may be perceived by the arranged Organ part, which is simply a nearly exact translation of the rest of the Score.

It remains only to say that it is with reading Scores as with everything else; time and study will lead to it insensibly if only we have a natural disposition for music.

Chapter IV.

The Mechanism of Accompaniment.

37. The talent of the accompanist consists in re-producing upon the pianoforte the intentions of the composer as exactly as possible. But difficulties of fingering, the want of variety in the sounds of the Pianoforte, a fault from which the orchestra is free, and the impossibility of making manifest the crossing parts, all this, I say, necessitates a change in certain passages in the accompaniment, and in the substitution of others more easy of execution, but still of an analogous nature.

38. It is useful to commence the study of accompaniment from Score with the works of Cimarosa, Paisiello, Guglielmi, and their immediate successors, because their style, though brilliant, is simple and clear. These works have the advantage of accustoming the accompanist to exactness without the necessity of making any very great efforts. It requires but small skill, in fact, to accompany without difficulty a piece written like the famous finale of "La Scuffiara," an opera by Paisiello, as may be seen from this fragment. Ex. 20.

It does not require much intelligence to see, upon

first looking at this Score, that the Violins and Oboes should be played with the right hand as far as the fifth measure in which the second Violin passes to the left hand. As to the Horns it is evident that they appertain to the latter. Thus this passage may be translated with facility in the following manner. Ex. 21.

Other compositions of this school and of this epoch present no greater difficulties either as to arrangement or fingering.

39. Many accompanists abuse the liberty which they possess of arranging the accompaniment in the most convenient manner for execution, and the most suitable to the instrument, changing the character of the passages sometimes from want of taste, sometimes through a certain sort of negligence. Reducing, for example, every kind of Arpeggio to that which we commonly call " batteries," they give to the music a monotony and a vulgar tone which destroys all its charm ; thus it is not an unfrequent occurrence that a passage like the following, Ex. 22, is accompanied in the following manner. Ex. 23.

It is not necessary to have any great musical organization to be struck with the want of taste displayed in such an arrangement. No doubt it would be very difficult to execute the accompaniment just as it is written ; that is to say, to keep the second Violin part in its exact form ; but it is quite possible to execute with the left hand a similar passage, as in the following example. Ex. 24.

Yet, if the design of the second Violin part is pro-longed through the whole of the piece, and above all if it modulates with any object, this system of accompaniment presents great difficulties, and forces the left hand to skip ; in this case it would be better to abandon the passage of the first Violin and to execute the part of the second Violin by the right hand in this manner.   Ex. 25.

40. The principal difficulty consists in judging promptly of that which may be advantageously given to the right or to the left hand.   These difficulties are independent of the number of orchestral parts that may happen to be in the Score ; sometimes a simple Quartet presents as many obstacles as a formidable Orchestra in consequence of the overlapping of the parts.   Nevertheless the works of the composers of the eighteenth century are generally sufficiently easy. Pergolesi and Durante are the models which are for the most part adopted.   The following passage will give an idea of their manner of writing in the sacred style, and of the manner in which the accompaniment should be arranged.   It is extracted from the " Salve Regina " of Pergolesi.   Ex. 26.

41. I have already said that there are compositions apparently simple which present considerable diffi-culty.   To give an example I take the opening of the " Ave maris stella " of Leo.   In the ritournelle of this piece the first Violin takes the melody, the second Violin and the Alto accompany with arpeggios of a certain kind, or with repeated chords (*baiteries*) full

of elegance, and the Bass is placed at a considerable distance. Ex. 27.

In all this there is much to embarrass the accompanist, and the exact execution of the music as it is written will be without effect. The accompaniment should therefore be limited to a simple left hand arpeggio, in which only the harmony and progression of the Bass is retained. Ex. 28.

42. As to the compositions of the modern school, particularly those of Mozart, of Cherubini, and of several other great musicians, they are often written with such an amount of intention that it is difficult to change the mode of accompaniment; thus, they present many great difficulties. The art of accompanying this music consists principally in allowing to pass alternatively from one hand to the other, certain passages which could not be executed by one hand alone. But this requires a considerable amount of skill, especially on account of the fingering. As an example of this kind of accompaniment I take the works of Cherubini, whose music is generally considered very difficult, because it was not composed at the pianoforte, and because everything is disposed to produce orchestral effects. I will imagine a wish to accompany the *Kyrie* from the *Mass for three voices in F*, of this composer, the commencement of which is as follows. Ex. 29.

At the first glance it is seen that the parts for the wind instruments are simply filling up, and that all the interest is in the Violins, Alto, and Bass. But the elegant form of the second Violin part does not permit the substitution of simple arpeggios nor of reiterated chords (*batteries*) and in order to preserve the features of the music it is necessary to play this part exactly as it is written. It becomes therefore necessary that the two hands alternatively occupy themselves with all that they can execute with facility : which they can in the following manner. Ex. 30.

No doubt there is some complication in this manner of accompaniment; but with perserverance it is possible to get accustomed to it. Farther, I know of no other manner of accompaniment, for I do not believe that anyone could possibly give the name of accompaniment to that which I have frequently heard. Ex. 31.

It is felt at once how tame this is, without its being necessary to analyze details.

43. Although certain passages are not easy to execute, they leave no doubt about the disposition of the parts in the two hands. This occurs when these are at a certain distance and do not cross. Ex. 32.

It is evident that the two Violin parts should be executed by the right hand, and the Alto by the left, during the first four bars, because the Alto part is too far off to be joined to the second Violin part. But at the fifth bar, the second Violin recedes from the first Violin and approaches the Alto, so that the left hand can take these two parts, leaving the first Violin part to the right hand. Ex. 33.

Without doubt there are great irregularities of fingering in this manner of accompaniment; but they are unavoidable. Farther, I do not believe that it is possible to curtail anything in accompaniment in this style.

44. Orchestral passages which are the most difficult to reproduce upon the pianoforte, are those in which the principal instruments approach and recede from each other rapidly, because it is necessary continually to pass the parts from one hand to the other. Of all authors Cherubini is he with whom this kind of difficulty is most frequently found. It is for this reason that his scores should be studied with the greatest care. The following is an example of such a passage, which I have taken from the opera of "*Elisa, ou le Mont St. Bernard.*" Ex. 34.

The necessity of giving one portion of the second Violin part to the right hand and another to the left, renders this passage very difficult, especially because of its rapidity. Still, this accompaniment should not be simplified, because the vocal part not being very prominent, the principal interest is in the Orchestral accompaniment. The accompanist is therefore obliged to arrange the passage as follows. Ex. 35.

45. The parts of the Violin, Alto, and Bass, frequently contain repeated notes in a quick movement; the execution of which would, upon a piano, not only be difficult, but destitute of effect. These repeated notes present themselves in different forms and are susceptible of many modifications in the

manner in which they should be executed upon the piano.

1st.—In recitatives, &c. These kinds of " Tremolo " are found disposed in the following manner. Ex. 36.

This may be arranged by the accompanist in several ways, the choice of which depends upon his caprice and upon his taste. Among the examples which I have given here, the first is suited to recitative ; the others appertain rather to measured accompaniment. Ex. 37.

2nd.—Sometimes the repeated notes are disposed in couples, as in the following examples. Ex. 38.

If the movement is rapid, the accompanist should simplify all the repeated notes thus. Ex. 39.

But if the movement is moderate, he should employ repetitions as in the following example. Ex. 40.

46. When the " Tremolo " occurs in the accompanying parts with a melody in one part, the Tremolo is given to the left hand, and the right hand takes the melody. Ex. 41.

47. The nature of the Piano not allowing the prolongation of sounds at will, as upon wind or stringed instruments ; it is evident that the long sounds which are sometimes found in scores would produce but a feeble effect, especially in slow movements, if the accompanist were to execute exactly that which is written. It is therefore necessary to arrange this kind of accompaniment by marking the different times of the measure. As to the mode of arrangement which should be adopted, it may be taken as a rule

that the smoothness which the composer has adopted in the accompaniment should be copied as nearly as possible, and the notes multiplied no more than necessary. Ex. 42.

In order to reproduce this accompaniment upon the pianoforte with the necessary quietude, the only means which can be employed is to take the harmony simply and to arrange it as follows. Ex. 43.

The taste more or less refined of the accompanist must indicate to him the system of accompaniment most suitable in like circumstances. These accompaniments are susceptible of as many varieties as there are possible characteristics of melody: for it is the nature of the melody which should guide the accompanist. It is evident that study and habit will teach more about matters of this kind than can be learned from any farther detail.

48. I have treated upon the points which have appeared to me the most important in the mechanism of accompaniment. But I have not the pretension to consider that I have said everything—who could say everything? If anyone undertook this it would be necessary to write volumes, the size of which would only spread discouragement. In order to be a good accompanist it is necessary to have, as for everything else connected with music, a good musical instinct. For persons thus gifted, these simple indications will suffice, but without such natural musical instinct, methods, volumes, and masters are useless.

Chapter V.

Concerning the influence of the Accompanist on the
Vocalist.

49. Vocalists are seldom people of the highest class,
independent of all outside influence, and deriving their
inspiration from their inner consciousness. The
greater part of them, on the other hand are under the
necessity of being guided in their intonations, excited
in their apathy, held back when they wish to go
forward, pressed forward when they drag. This is
especially true of singers of part-music, in which the
faults of one are taken up and imitated by others.

It is the business of the accompanist to regulate the
execution. He should influence, and never be in-
fluenced. For this reason, he should study the
character of the vocalists whom he accompanies, and
whom he directs, according to their weak or strong
points. Those who, when accompanied with exactness
and coldness, have no expression in their singing, may
have their enthusiasm roused. Those who go beyond
all reasonable bounds may be calmed down by the
coolness of the accompanist. From this, the re-
sponsibility of the accompanist may be imagined, also
til which may be justly expected from him.

50. When the accompanist perceives that the vocalist has not a true intonation, he should allow him to hear the melody, allowing it to predominate in the accompaniment, and even in certain cases slightly anticipating the notes of the melody. But this must be done with skill and care in order that the vocalist alone may perceive the intention.

51. Almost all musicians accelerate quick movements, and retard those which are slow. From the influence of mutual excitement, they finish by rendering the Allegro beyond all power of execution, and the Adagio sluggish. The accompanist should take particular notice of these two contrary effects. It is necessary that he should be firm in his time, and that the vocalists should perceive his firmness. This perception will make them careful to keep the original time.

Amongst great singers, as amongst great instrumentalists, there are many who, from a false feeling of expression, keep retarding and accelerating alternatively; the Italians of the new school, who are ignorant of the effect of strict time, generally follow this system. If they were forced to maintain strict time, the result would be coldness in their singing, they would be deprived of all their inspirations. When an accompanist perceives this tendency in a singer, he should yield to him, because opposition would be purely useless, and would establish between himself and the vocalist a kind of antagonism, the result of which could only be disagreeable. It is

therefore necessary to foresee all the intentions of the
vocalist, and to second those intentions as far as
possible.   This art has its difficulties.

Other grand vocalists, on the contrary, require the
accompaniment to be to a certain extent a *Métronome*,
to serve as a rallying point; and on this unalterable
time they base all the retardations and anticipations
which their imagination suggests to them, taking
particular care always to hit upon the precise time
whenever that becomes necessary.   Such were Garat
and Crescentini; such is, according to common opinion,
Tamburini.   This mode of expression is no doubt
the right mode; but for its exercise a very happy
organisation is necessary.

This method presents a certain amount of difficulty
to the accompanist, because he is liable to be influ-
enced by the apparent defect of time ; but the necessary qualities for accompanying are only to be
acquired by great practice and experience.

SECOND SECTION.—On Style of Accompaniment.

Chapter VI.

On Difference of Style.

52. Each musical epoch has its own characteristics which must be known in order to conform to them in the accompaniment. Musical epochs may be divided as follows:—1. The contrapuntal style, without accompaniment, known as the style *alla Palestrina*. 2. That of music with figured Bass accompaniment, from Carissimi to Durante. 3. That of the music of the middle of the 18th century, divided into the Italian, German, and French styles. 4. That of music since Haydn and Mozart until the present time, in which the difference of style is divided by imperceptible shades.

The art of the accompanist consists in knowing well the characteristics of each epoch and of each particular style in order to avoid the introduction of any foreign matter. This is especially important in music which has only the accompaniment of a figured

Bass, upon which the accompanist has to extem-
porise.

53. It is also necessary that the accompanist should
understand the different movements indicated by the
same words during different epochs.   The andante of
Durante or of Pergolesi is slower than that of
Rossini and Beethoven; the allegro on the contrary
is quicker.   Generally the slow movements of the old
schools were slower than those of the modern school,
but the quick movements less quick.

54. In the following chapters I shall treat of the
accompaniment of the various styles of music. As to
that of the fugued style, or contrapuntal style of
Palestrina, his predecessors and successors, the vocal
parts must be reproduced upon the pianoforte without
the addition of any filling up of the harmony, and
without the introduction of any strange ornament.

Suppose that it is required to sustain the voices
with the pianoforte or organ in the *Credo* of the Mass
Ecce Sacerdos Magnus of Palestrina, of which this is
the commencement.   Ex. 44.

The four parts should be executed upon the pianoforte as they are written, in the following manner.
Ex. 45.

This example will suffice; for all music of this
kind must be executed in the same manner.

Chapter VII.

On the Accompaniment of Early Music without Orchestra. The duets and trios of Clari, Durante, Handel, and the Psalms of Marcello.

55. Nothing is apparently more easy than to accompany the compositions of Scarlatti, Clari, Durante, and Marcello, which have only a figured Bass accompaniment. Anyone would think that it was sufficient to know the rules of harmony in order to play the accompaniments perfectly. But there are certain traditions which should be known, to impart to the accompaniment of this kind of music the characteristics which the authors had in view in its composition. It is now my intention to speak about these traditions.

56. It must be remembered, in the first place, that the cantatas for a single voice, duets, trios, and all the music not written for four voices, was never in Italy accompanied in more than three parts. This accompaniment was not a chord accompaniment (plaqué) according to the custom in France, but was figurated (figuré) as it is called, that is to say, singing through all the parts.

In the case of a duet or a trio, in order to figurate or harmonize the accompaniment, it is sufficient to

follow with the eye the different voices and to reproduce them upon the pianoforte in such a manner as
to obtain some imitation of them, and for the rest to
confine oneself to the harmony, as in the following
example. Ex. 46.

57. When the entries of the voices are at considerable distances in duets, or when we have to deal with
a cantata for a single voice, the indications of imitation of movement, or of rhythm, being more rare, the
accompanist must rely upon himself rather than that
which is written, and this demands more skill. The
following example, taken from the duets of Durante,
will show how, by means of imitations of rhythm, an
accompaniment of this nature is made interesting.
Ex. 47.

58. This old music, which has no other accompaniment than an organ part, formerly called Thorough Bass (*Basse Continue*) often has also Basses
for the symphonies. If these symphonies are not
figured, or if with them we meet with the words
" Tasto Solo," it is necessary to be careful about accompanying them with harmony in the right hand,
because the austerity of a bass solo frequently
entered into the plan of these compositions.

But if the symphony is figured, it is necessary to
examine the design of the movement in order to see
if there is not room for some imitation of its style,
and if in the movement any kind of facility is dis-
covered for the augmentation of effect, it is necessary
to profit by the discoveries. For example, the Sym-

phony to the 18th Psalm of Marcello appears at first sight to be a veritable Tasto Solo. Ex. 48.

But after an attentive examination of this symphony, and of the character of the piece to which it serves as introduction, it is plainly perceptible that it may be treated as follows. Ex. 49.

59. I believe that I have no need to add anything to that which I have already said in this chapter; *viz.*, that in accompanying any three parts it is necessary to pay great attention to perfect purity of harmony; this principle is known by all who have learned the rules of Harmony and Thorough Bass.

All the observations which have been made are applicable to the duets and trios of Clari, Steffani, Durante; to the cantatas of Scarlatti, and of Handel; also to all the authors contemporary with those great musicians.

Chapter VIII.

On the Reproduction of Ancient Orchestral Accompaniments.

60. The dramatic and religious music of the ancient masters present few difficulties of execution ; as the orchestration is so simple. The principal merit of the accompanist is exactness. I use this word in the utmost fulness of its meaning.

Frequently the accompaniment of this kind of music is only written in two parts. At the present time this appears thin and ineffective, but this defect itself is characteristic of these compositions ; and it is necessary above all things to preserve the characteristics of each epoch. A great error would be committed if anyone fancied that this old music could be enriched by filling up the harmony of the chords, as I have sometimes heard these scores filled up by accompanists. When passages similar to the following occur, they should be accompanied as they are written. Ex. 50.

The oratorios of Handel, and several other compositions in which the bass, being figured, indicates an obbligato organ part, are exceptions to this rule. The orchestration consisting only of two parts, it is necessary in this case to fill up the harmony in the best manner possible. Ex. 51.

61. The chief merit in accompanying this music consists in the expression given to it, although the melodic forms are old. The word expression has two different meanings; the first concerns a certain accentuation, by means of which the impressions of grief, pleasure, love, &c., are manifested. This meaning of the word belongs to all times, it never changes, and it is of this that I wish to speak here. The other is simply the tradition of certain generally received forms, which paint a variety of sentiments, more or less rich, subject to changes in fashion. Some of these forms had a certain effect when the public had a clue to their meaning, but at present leave the hearer cold and uninfluenced, because the tradition concerning them is lost, and because musicians know not the mode of execution suited to them.

A good accompanist should never neglect any of the means which tend to augment the effect of the music; he should be well acquainted with all forms and all traditions. Those of the older music of which I speak here are very simple. They consist, when the same phrase is repeated, in executing *forte* the first time, *piano* the second time in some cases, and to do the very opposite in others. This is that which the accompanist ought to know, because the ancient composers frequently neglected to indicate these changes, as they were at that time generally understood. Ex. 52.

Not one of these changes is indicated in the score of Pergolesi, but every accompanist acquainted with the tradition concerning it will know what to do.

62. In all airs and duets, the motion of which is quick, the custom was to play the symphonies forcibly, and upon the entry of the vocal part to soften the tone. There is in this method something grand and majestic, producing a very fine effect, which the accompanist should not neglect. The following is an example of great beauty taken from the cantata, "*Orpheus,*" by the same author. Ex. 53.

63. The recitative in all compositions of this epoch is simply accompanied by a figured bass like that of the Italian comic operas. The accompanist should execute the harmony indicated by the figures, without regarding the time, but merely following the singer. At the commencement of the recitative, and especially where there is any modulation, the notes of the chord which indicate the key should be played in arpeggio. These arpeggios also, should just in the slightest degree precede the singer in order to facilitate his intonation. Ex. 54.

64. That species of recitative which is called Free recitative (recitatif libre) has remained very nearly that which it was in the epoch in which it was invented ; but another species has since been produced, known as the recitative obbligato (recitatif obligé), which is accompanied by the orchestra, and interrupted by symphonies. From the time of Jomelli until that of Rossini, this kind of recitative had only

been employed in the most important scenes of serious operas. But the master of Pesaro, in imitation of Gluck and the French composers of his school, has introduced the obbligato recitative entirely through his Italian serious operas.

In the recitative obbligato the symphonies are played with a measured movement, and the accompanist follows the singer in the other parts. But though the symphonies are thus played, the motion is accelerated or retarded according to the sentiment which they are intended to express. The indications of these changes of movement are frequently wanting in the scores ; the accompanist should supply them by his own intelligence, or from the traditions attaching to them. We shall see farther on that the recitative of Gluck is, to a greater extent than any other, varied by these changes of movement.

The following is one of the most beautiful models of obbligato recitative of the ancient school. It is taken from the *Allessandro nell' Indie* of Piccini. Ex. **55.**

CHAPTER IX.

On the Modern Style of Accompaniment.

1. *The Operas of Gluck.*

65. Music is capable of an infinity of modifications, which have all their peculiar beauties and defects. Men of genius who originate a style are ordinarily dominated by exclusive ideas, and by a conviction which is at once the cause of their success and the precursor of the oblivion into which their works are destined to fall. They only see one side of their art, and concentrate upon this all the faculties of their soul and mind ; but by so doing they neglect the other sides. Gluck is a striking example of this speciality, which is one of the characteristics of genius. Dramatic expression pushed to the extreme limits of possibility was the object of his labours. Everything which tended to this end, according to his ideas, was treated with particular care ; everything else he neglected. But although, as far as purity of harmony is concerned, he left much to be desired in his productions, yet as to melody, regularity of phrases, and the employment of instruments, his inspirations are so imposing, his recitative is so true, his expression is so varied, and his orchestral effects have so much

originality, that he stands in the first rank of dramatic composers.

66. Upon looking at a score of Gluck, it is almost impossible to form an idea of the effect which it is capable of producing, unless it has previously been heard. In the disposition of his voices and instruments there is an indescribable appearance of lack of skill, which strikes one at first ; but upon hearing the work executed, it is astonishing to find that by this apparent awkwardness, effects of the greatest power are produced. This is one of this musician's peculiarities.

Gluck is also the composer who has most frequently employed momentary variations of movement ; and as he has neglected to indicate these variations in his scores, tradition alone has preserved them to the present time. Unfortunately this tradition gets weaker from day to day, and at last it will be lost, because the répertoire of this great artist is disappearing little by little from the scene. Nothing will then remain but the feeling, more or less delicate, of the executants, in order that they may be revived at some future time. The impossibility of entering here into such details as might preserve them, without passing the limits of my work, forces me to confine myself to certain general observations.

67. Until the time of Gluck, composers had but one object in view, the melody as a principal part, the narmony as accessory ; or the exact opposite, as in the school of Bach and Handel. Expression was

understood, but not that which is known at the present
time as the music of effect (la musique d'effet).   Gluck
appears to me to have been the first who conceived
that which we understand by this phrase ; his scores
are, at all events, the oldest in which are to be found
dispositions of effect, independent of the melody or
combinations of learned harmony.   The difficulties of
the art of accompaniment upon the pianoforte have
also greatly increased since the epoch in which he
wrote his French operas, for he did not deem it necessary to limit himself to the mere sustaining of the
voices by a correct execution of a simple harmony, in
the manner of his predecessors ; thus it is indispensable that the accompanist should possess good taste,
capable of choosing the most telling effects, and
imagining the means of reproducing them properly
upon the pianoforte.   Before Gluck, the best accompanist was he who put himself into the shade ; but
since the revolution which Gluck effected, the accompaniment has become a too important part of the
general harmony to escape due prominence.   I shall
choose as an example the recitative of the High Priest
consulting the Oracle, in the first act of *Alceste*, a
grand conception, unlike anything which had pre-
ceded it.   The first object of the accompanist should
be to reproduce as vividly as possible the grandeur
and majesty of this scene.   There is not one single
unimportant note in all that Gluck has written in this
admirable recitative ; everything ought to be felt,
everything ought to be expressed ; no honour would

be due to him who could accompany in a dry and cold manner such a scene as this. I shall endeavour to show what should be done, in order as nearly as possible, to reproduce upon the piano the effect of the orchestra; but it should not be forgotten that there is one essential which cannot be written: that is the sentiment, the soul which animates the note when the exponent possesses a highly sensitive organisation. I shall, therefore, not be able to give, with all my efforts, more than an imperfect idea of the effect of this passage to those who cannot supply what is wanting by their own feeling. Ex. 56.

It is evident that the accompanist should have plenty of tact and intelligence, and at the same time, great strength of feeling, in order to reproduce upon the pianoforte these great effects. Of these qualities I cannot give any just idea, either by notes or by words; the accompanist must possess them, otherwise he lacks that which is most essential. With these qualities, it is possible to became a *remarkable* accompanist; without them it is only possible by labour to become an *exact* accompanist.

68. It is often by the employment of the most simple means that Gluck produces his most beautiful effects. For instance, in the scene of *Iphigenie*, in which Agamemnon deplores the fate of his daughter, there occurs one passage in which the hautboy expresses by isolated notes the agony of paternal love. To look at the score, the hautboy part does not appear to be of any great importance; but it is

necessary that an accompanist should learn to perceive the power of passages of this kind, when he is dealing with the music of a composer who puts aside rules and ordinary methods. It is necessary, in fact, that he should make an oboe of his piano. The passage is as follows. Ex. 57.

69. Volumes might be written if I wished to continue my analysis of the works of this great artist with a view to correct execution, but such is not my intention at present. I have simply wished to render intelligible all which I understand by the phrase, "*music of effect*," and to indicate to beginners that which should be the object of their attention and of their studies when they undertake to accompany the operas of a musician, who, for the first time, knew how to utilize the resources of the orchestra.

70. Piccini, Sacchini and Salieri, whose French works were either contemporary with, or immediate successors to those of Gluck, are less difficult to accompany. First, because the objects are more manifest; second, because the means employed are more regular and less original, although these composers were distinguished by particular qualities, notably by melodies better conceived and better phrased than those of Gluck.

2. *On Paisiello, Cimarosa, and their School.*

71. Each great composer has his own particular style, the spirit of which it is necessary to grasp, in order properly to accompany his works.

This style consists, not only in quality of ideas and in the nature of the melody, but also upon the instrumentation. To produce the proper effect every detail must be observed; nothing must be neglected.

72. The music of Paisiello is sweet, expressive, elegant, and often impassioned. His orchestration is simple and somewhat thin, for it contains rarely more than the quartett, two Oboes, and two Horns; but it is almost always so disposed as to produce telling effects. Even in the smallest detail he exhibits a delicate feeling, with which the accompanist should be in perfect sympathy in accompanying his works.

When the style of the scores of the *Molinara*, *Nina*, *Roi Theodore* and the duet from *L'Olimpiade* have been perceived, the master will be better understood, and his music accompanied successfully. Farther, his scores do not offer any difficulties of mechanism in their accompaniment. If only anyone can read well he is not likely to have any trouble with the music of Paisiello. Facility in reading is a great matter, but of course it is not everything.

73. The orchestration of Cimarosa is richer than that of Paisiello, but offers no greater difficulties to the accompanist; it possesses, however, a greater variety of effect. But as there is an infinity of soul in the details, and of the spirit in the essential parts, it is necessary that the accompanist should put more lightness and brilliancy into its execution than is necessary in his accompaniments of the works of Paisiello. It will suffice to study with care the duet of the *Matri-*

E

*mo*nio *Segreto*, " *Cara, cara*," the Air, " *Udite tutti,
udite*," the Quartett, " *Sento in petto un fredo gelo*,"
the Air, " *Pria che spunti*," and the Finale of the first
act of the same Opera, also to grasp the style of
these, in order to know thoroughly the style of this
composer.

74. Though the ideas of Fioravanti were frequently
commonplace he produced a considerable amount of
effect, because no one has better disposed than he
the return of the principal phrases and the essential
parts of the composition. This characteristic gives a
spirit to his music, which is extremely fascinating,
especially in the finales. The accompanist should be
attentive to this quality, and show by the warmth and
spirit of his execution that he understands the intention of the composer. The orchestration offers
no material difficulty in reproduction upon the
pianoforte.

3. *On Gretry, Monsigny, Dalayrac, &c.*

75. We are aware that it is not by their instrumentation that these composers of the French school
have rendered themselves celebrated. Their merit
consisted in the truth of their declamation, the spirit
of their dialogue, the grace of their melody, and the
just feeling by which they were always animated.
But their works require attention, because they are
incorrectly written, especially those of Gretry and
Monsigny, and because their Basses are frequently
bad. These two composers were ignorant of music ;

but as they worked instinctively, they have sometimes hit upon orchestral effects so happy that they must not be neglected.

It would be an error to attempt to correct the bareness and even the faults which are to be found in the music of these composers ; all this is part of the individual characteristic of their music, a characteristic which should be preserved with care, because this alone gives life to works of art.

Chapter **X.**

———

On Mozart, Cherubini, Méhul, Spontini, Rossini, and the Modern School.

76. When we get to Mozart, we are completely in the domain of the music of effect. This is not the place in which to speak of the immense genius, and of the prodigious qualities of this great man. I merely remark that it is he who has introduced almost all the instrumental effects which are adopted in our time, and which the skill of instrumentalists and the perfection of instruments have farther developed. It is he, above all, who first gave to wind instruments their present importance in the orchestra. The effects which he drew from them are magical, and require on the part of the accompanist, a considerable amount of sagacity and experience, in order to reproduce them upon the pianoforte in a manner analagous to the idea of the composer. They are so multiform, so varied, that they defy all analysis.

The skill acquired by degrees, good natural talent, and continual practice, these alone can teach us all that is necessary to be known. *Don Juan*, the *Noces de Figaro*, and the *Flute enchanté*, are three types of different effects, to which it is impossible to give too great an amount of study.

77. Cherubini and Méhul are very similar to Mozart in their manner of instrumentation, but with certain shadings which characterize their genius. The close and elegant progression of the parts renders the music of Cherubini more difficult to accompany than any other; but upon becoming accustomed to his manner of writing, his effects may be reproduced successfully upon the pianoforte.

78. The music of Méhul is full of imitations, which produce their effect upon instruments of different quality of tone, but which, upon the pianoforte, are hardly reproducible, the effort of their attempted reproduction being fatiguing both for the vocalist and for the auditor. His instrumentation can therefore be frequently simplified without any destruction of the effect of his music. This author has a great power of dramatic expression, which it is necessary that the accompanist should fully realize in order to reproduce the composer's intentions.

79. Spontini took Gluck for his model, adding to his peculiar style the richness of orchestration from which he sometimes drew great effects, but which is sometimes simply a puerile exhibition, and often incorrect. The principal task of the accompanist in executing the music of Spontini must be to discard everything useless, and to choose that which is, from that which is not, essential. In *La Vestale*, and in *Fernand Cortez*, are to be found passages of great dramatic expression, which demand a considerable

amount of care, intelligence and true feeling on the part of the accompanist.

80. There are few who have found so many ways of producing new effects as Rossini. By transferring to the wind instruments, and especially to the brass, the styles of accompaniment before used only for stringed instruments, he changed the entire character of the orchestra, and an infinite number of new effects resulted from these combinations. Yet his scores are not very difficult to accompany; only they do not allow the accompanist to rest in security, because at every moment, we find unexpected effects.

81. The necessity of discerning the intention of the authors, of imagining the means by which these intentions are to be reproduced upon the pianoforte, and of making everything clear in the execution, should never give to the accompaniment the appearance of labour and difficulty.

As I have said before, there are other duties to be fulfilled, the vocalists are to be guided, kept in true time, and aided in their intonation. These duties cannot be performed unless the mind is untroubled. To be calm and full of life and spirit at the same time, that is the problem for resolution.

CHAPTER XI.

Conclusion.

82. I cannot better terminate these instructions on the art of Accompaniment than by indicating the order which should be followed in the reading and reproduction of the scores which will educate at the same time the eyes, the intelligence, and the taste.

In the first place, works without orchestral accompaniments having only a figured bass should be taken in the following order :—

1. The Duets of Steffani.
2. The Duets and Trios of Clari.
3. The Duets of Handel and Durante.
4. The Cantatas of Alexandro Scarlatti.
5. The Psalms of Marcello.

The next works for study are the religious compositions of the Italian masters in the order indicated beneath :—

1. The " Salve Regina " and " Stabat Mater " of Pergolesi.

2. The "Alma redemptoris" and "Ave regina cœlorum" of Leo.

3. The Litanies of Durante.

4. The "Miserere" and Offertories of Jomelli.

5. The Oratorios of Handel.

The following sacred compositions with orchestral accompaniments should follow :—

1. The Masses, Motetts and Vespers of Durante and Jomelli.

2. The Masses of Haydn, Mozart, &c.

3. The Short Te Deum of Handel.

The scores of operas should be studied in the following order :—

1. The Works of Jomelli, Trajetta, Galuppi, and the Italian Opera Scores of Piccini, Sacchini, &c.

2. The Operas of Philidor, Monsigny, Grétry, and Dalayrac.

3. The French Operas of Piccini, Sacchini, Salieri, &c.

4. The Scores of Gluck.

5. The Works of Paisiello, Cimarosa, Fioravanti, Mayr, Paer, Nicolo, Isouard, &c.

6. The Operas of Mozart, the Requiem of the same composer, the Scores of Méhul, Berton, Catel, Cherubini, Spontini, Rossini, &c.

Ex. 1.
Unison.
or
Unison.
Ex. 2.
Piccolo.
Effect.
Ex. 3.
Clarionet in B flat.
Effect.
Ex. 4.
Clarionet in A.
Effect.
Ex. 5.
Clarionet in B flat.
Real pitch.
Mode of execution.
Ex. 6.
English Horn.
Effect.
Ex. 7.
2 Horns in C.
Effect.
Ex. 8.
Horns in D.
Effect.
Imagine the Key C on the 3rd line.
Horns in E flat.
Effect.
Imagine the Key F on the 4th line (Bass Clef) and play an octave higher.
Horns in E.
Effect.
Suppose the F clef as before but substitute 4 sharps for 3 flats.
Horns in F.
Effect.
Imagine the Key C on the 2nd line.
Horns in G.
Effect.
Imagine the Key F on the 4th line and play an octave higher.
Horns in A.
Effect.
Imagine the Key C on the 1st line.
Horns in B flat.
Effect.
Imagine the Key C on the 4th line and play an octave higher.
Horns in B flat below.
Effect.
Imagine the Key C on the 4th line and play at the indicated pitch.

Ex. 9.

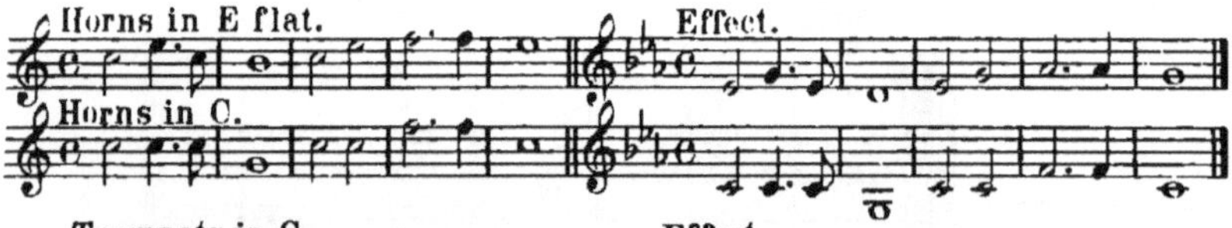

Ex. 10.

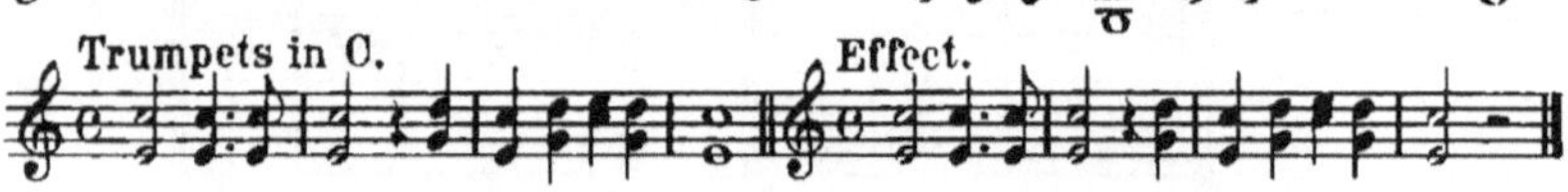

Ex. 11.

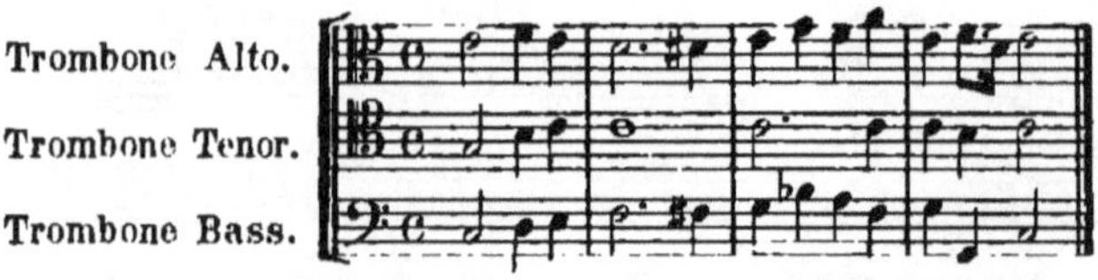

Ex. 12.

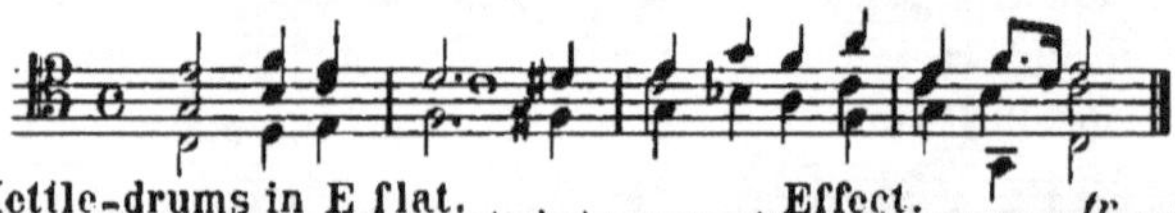

Ex. 13.

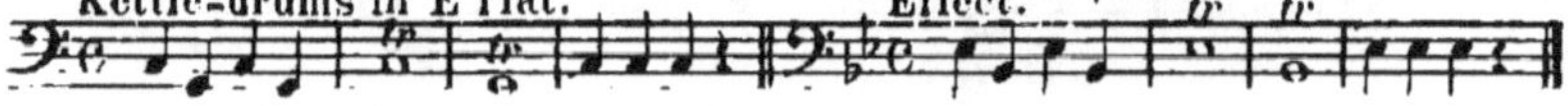

Ex. 14.

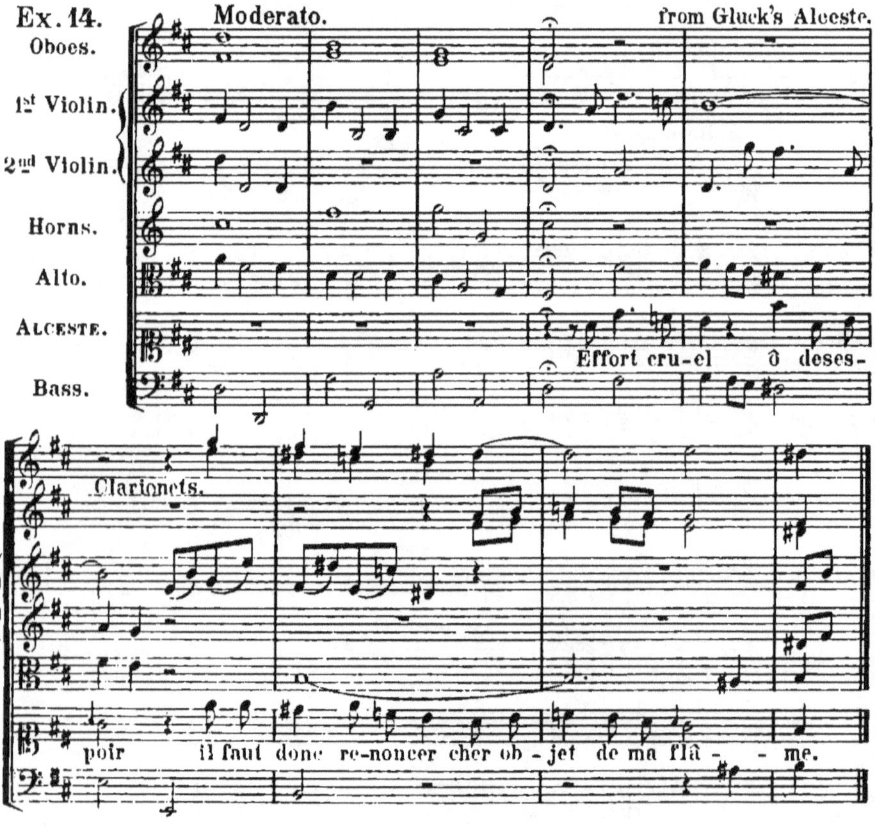

Ex. 15.
1st Violin.
2nd Violin.
Alto.
Bass.

Ex. 16.

Ex. 17.
Allegro vivace.
1st Violin.
2nd Violin.
Viola.
Oboes.
Horns in D.

Do — — na no — bis pa — cem

Do — — na

Bass and Organ.

pa - - - cem, pa - cem,
no - bis pa - cem, pa - - - - - -
Do - - - na
Do - - - na no - bis pa - cem,
do - na no - - - bis,
- cem do - na
no - bis pa - cem, pa - - - cem,

Ex. 18.

London, W. Reeves.

Ex. 19.

Beethoven, Op. 123.

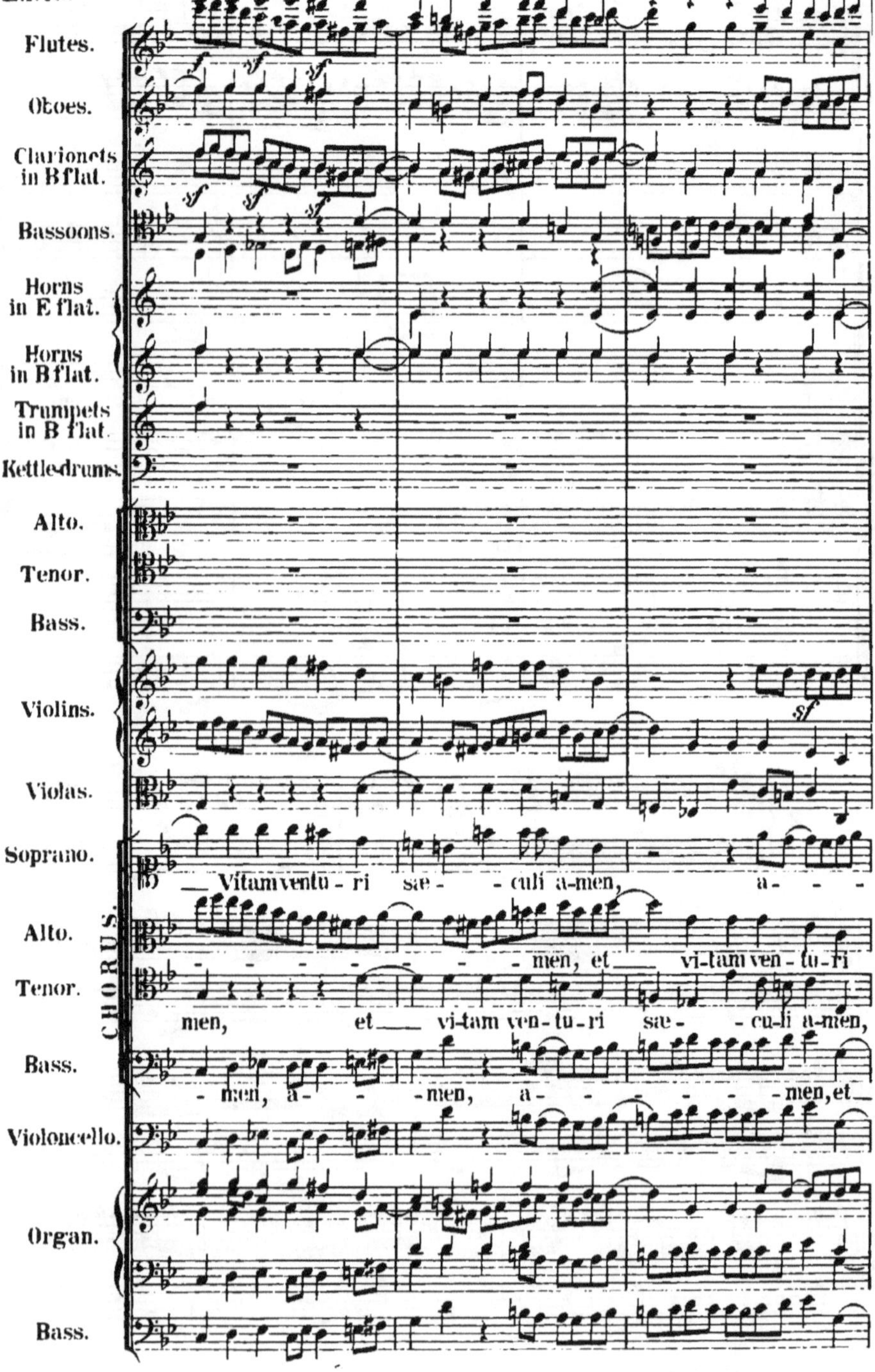

- - men, a - men, et vi-tam ventu-ri

ia - men, a-men, a-men, a-men, et vi-tam ven -

-tu-ri sæ - culi a - men, a - - men,

Ex. 20.

Moderato.
Violins.
Oboes.
Horns in D.
Alto.
Madame.
Chiarina.
Ninetta.
Bass.
Madame.
Mie raggazze favo - ri-te
favorite favo - ri-te.
Ninetta.
Deh! scu-tate
com - pa - ti-te.
Chiarina.
Lo con-
fesso
v'ho man-ca-te.
Madame.
Non s pensa più al pas-sa-to.

Ex. 21. PIANO.

Ex. 22. Moderato. Violins. Alto. Voice. Bass.

Caro o-get - to del mio a - mo - re non te-

me - te fa - te co - - re

Ex. 23. VOICE.

Caro o-get - to del mio a - mo - re non te-

PIANO.

me - te fa - te co - - re

Fetis, How to play from Score.

London, W. Reeves.

Ex. 24.

VOICE.

Caro o-get - to del mio a - mo - re non te-

PIANO.

me - te fa - to co - re

Ex. 25.

VOICE.

Caro o-get - to del mio a - mo - re non te-

PIANO.

me - te fa - to co - re

Ex. 26.

Violins.

Alto.

Voice.

Bass.

Sal - ve, sal - ve Re-gina

Manner of accompanying this passage.

VOICE.

PIANO.

Sal - ve, sal - ve Regi-na

Larghetto maestoso.

Ex. 29.

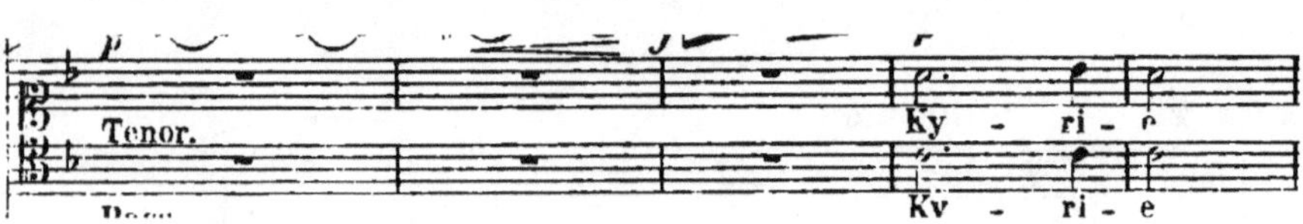
Tenor.
Ky - ri - e
Ky - ri - e

Ex. 30. Sostenuto. PIANO.

Ex. 31. PIANO.

Ex. 32. Violins. Alto. Voice. Violoncello and C.B.

Andante con moto. From the same Mass by Cherubini.

Lau-damus.

Ex. 33. PIANO.

Ex. 34.

Flutes.
Oboes.
Clarinets.
Bassoons.
Violins.
Alto.
Florindo.

Quoi!   c'est el - - le et

Bass.

mon _____ a - mi   que me font

Ex. 35.

PIANO.

Ex. 36.

Violins.

Alto.

Bass.

Ex. 37.

PIANO.

Ex. 38.

Violins.

Alto.

Bass.

Ex. 39.

PIANO.

Ex. 40.

PIANO.

Ex. 41.

Violins.

Allegro

Ex. 43.

Di - let-ta im - ma-gi-ne del mio con-sor - te

Ex. 44.

Pa - trem om ni - po - ten-tem,

Pa - trem om - ni - po - ten - tem,

Pa -

om - ni - po - ten - tem

om - ni - po - ten - tem

Ec -

trem om - ni - po - ten - tem fac-

fac-to-rem cœ - li et ter - ræ

fac - to-rem cœ - li et ter - ræ vi - si

cœ sa

torem cœ - li et ter - ræ vi -

Ex. 45.

Ex. 46.

PIANO.

Cantando un dì se de a Laurin da al fonte

Cantando un dì se de a Laurin da al
36 36 6 7 7 3

sot-to ver-di al - lo-ri qui negli es-ti-vi ar-

fon-te sot-to ver-di al-lo-ri qui negli es-
6 46 6 3
6 9 6

dori l'au - - re so a vi al zef-

ti - viar-dori l'au - - re so a vi al
+4 6 6 6

- - - - - fi ro chie de - a

zef - - - - - fi ro chie de - a
6
4

Ex. 47.

PIANO.
An-da - te, an-da te o miei sospi -
- ri o miei sospi - ri al cor d'Ire-ne
An-da - te, anda - te o miei so-
spi-ri o miei so-spi-ri al cor d'I-rene
An-da - te, anda -
andate, an-
te, an-da - te o miei so - spi - - ri o miei so-spi - - ri al cor d'i-
da-te, an-da - - te o miei sospi - - ri o miei sospi - -

Ex. 48.

Ex. 49.

PIANO.

Cieli im-men-si nar-ra no del grande iddi - - o la glo-ri-a

Cieli im-men-si narra no del grande id-dio la glo-ri-a

Cieli im-men-si nar-ra no del gran-de id-dio la glo-ri-a

Cieli im-men-si nar-ra no del gran-de id - dio la glo-ri-a

Cieli im-men-si nar-ra no del gran-de id - dio la glo-ri-a

Ex. 50. **Andante.**

Violins.

Alto.

Bass.

Ex. 51.

From Handel's Messiah.

Violins.

Voice.

Organ.

PIANO

Get thee up in to the high moun - tain

Example of this kind of expression taken from Pergolesi's "Stabat Mater."

Ex. 52.

Et tre - me - bat cum vi - de - bat na - ti

poe - nas na - ti poe - nas — in - - cli - ti

et tre - me bat cum vi - de bat na - ti

poe - nas na - ti poe - nas — in - - cli - ti

Ex. 53. Presto.

Violins.

Alto.

Voice.

Bass.

Presto.

PIANO.

London, W. Reeves

Ex. 54.

O d'Euri-di-ce n'an-drò fas-to-so, n'an-drò fas-to-so

Voice.

Si che pietà non v'è se ame non lice piegar del fato il braccio onde ri-

Bass.

PIANO.

sa-ni la cruda pie-ga d'Eu-ri-di-ce in se-no non v'è pie-tà

nò non s'intende amore se in van sos - pi-ro in van mi crucio e piango.

Ex. 55. Largo.

Allegro.

E questo il modo sos-pi-ra-to da no-i quest'è la

pace quest'e il regno fe-li-ce

f Allegro.

*) Here is one of those passages in which the accompanist, though he has no indica-
tion of change of movement, should rise in intensity of feeling, with the vocalist. Examples similar to this are frequent in Obbligato Recitative.

Ex.56.

Flutes.

Oboes.

Clarinets.

Violins.

Alto.

The
High-Priest.

Bass.

PIANO.

sible a nos gemisse-ments

tains m'en donnent l'assu-rance

plein de l'esprit di

\- te   en - tou - re la statu-e

tel
tout m'annon - ce du
cresc.
Dieu la présen - ce su - prê - me ce Dieu sur nos destine veut

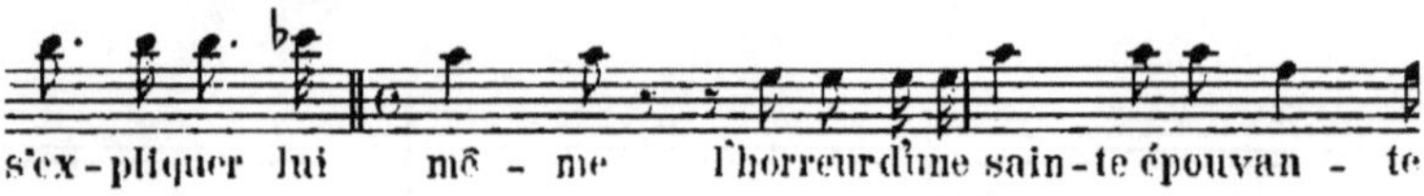
s'ex-pliquer lui mê - me l'horreur d'une sain-te épouvan - te

la ter - re sous mes pas   fuit et se préci -

pi - te

_ff_

_ff_

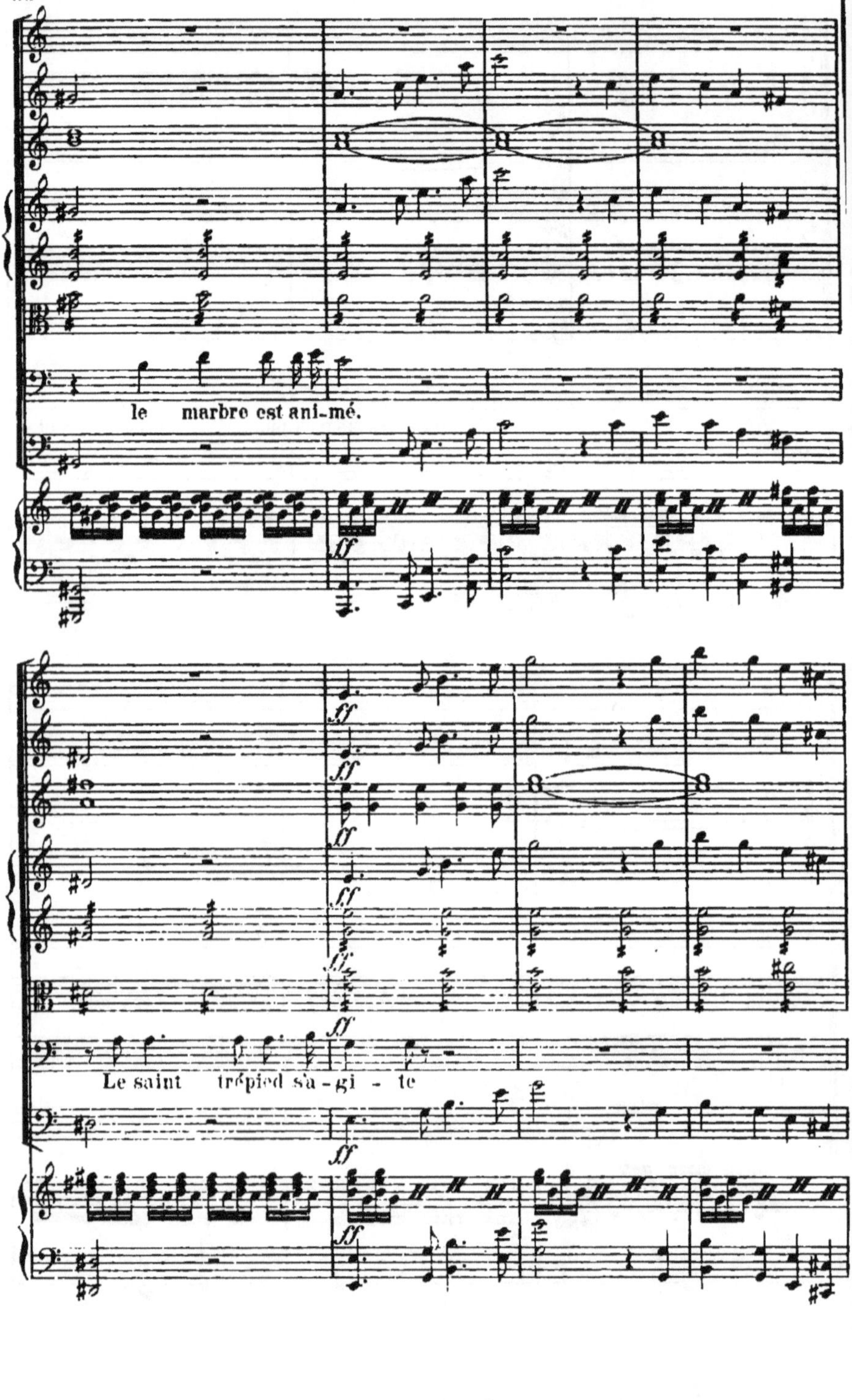
le marbre est ani-mé.
ff
Le saint trépied s'a-gi - te

tout se remplit d'un juste ef-froi.

Il va par - ler saisi de crainte et de res-pect

peuple   ob-serve un profond si - lence   Rei - ne   dépose a son as-

con espress.

pect   le vain orgueil   de la puis-san - ce   trem - - - ble.

Ex. 57.

Moderato.

Violins. Alto. Oboe. Agamemnon. Bass. Piano.

J'entends reten-tir dans mon

sein le cri plaintif de la na-tu-re el-le par-le à mon

coeur et sa voix est plus su-re que les o - ra-cles

du des-tin que les o - ra-cles du des-tin.

cresc.